HEALING FROM
INFIDELITY

How To Regain and Rebuild Trust After You or Your Partner Cheats

Lola Martins

TABLE OF CONTENTS

INTRODUCTION

In the idyllic town of Oakridge, Stephen and Alyssa were the epitome of a picture-perfect couple. Their love story had flourished over the years, bound by trust and a deep connection. However, their world was shaken to its core when Stephen's path unexpectedly crossed with that of Ariana, a captivating and enigmatic woman.

Drawn into a web of temptation, Stephen found himself entangled in a brief affair with Ariana. Overwhelmed by guilt and remorse, he confessed his infidelity to Alyssa, bracing himself for the potential end of their once-unbreakable bond.

Heartbroken and betrayed, Alyssa faced a tumultuous internal battle. She struggled to reconcile the image of the man she loved with the one who had strayed. Yet, deep down, she recognized that their relationship was worth fighting for, and she yearned to find a way back to the love they had built.

Together, Stephen and Alyssa embarked on a journey of healing, guided by their unwavering commitment to each other. They sought the support of a compassionate therapist, who provided them with the tools and strategies to rebuild their relationship from the ground up.

In the face of adversity, Stephen demonstrated true remorse and an unwavering dedication to earning back Alyssa's trust. He embraced vulnerability, openly sharing his innermost struggles and taking full responsibility for his actions. Recognizing the importance of transparency, he became an open book, allowing Alyssa to heal at her own pace and ask the difficult questions that gnawed at her heart.

Alyssa, on her part, embarked on a personal journey of self-discovery and self-care. She dug deep within herself, finding the strength to confront her own fears, insecurities, and doubts. Through introspection, she discovered her own resilience and the capacity to forgive—a powerful testament to her love for Stephen.

With time, patience, and an unyielding commitment to growth, Stephen and Alyssa slowly rebuilt the shattered foundation of their relationship. They embarked on new rituals of trust-building, such as open and honest communication, rebuilding intimacy, and creating shared goals for their future. They also found solace in cultivating new passions together, reigniting the spark that had once defined their love.

Their journey was far from easy, marked by setbacks and moments of doubt. However, armed with their unwavering love, resilience, and a shared vision of a future stronger than their past, Stephen and Alyssa defied the odds. Through their collective efforts, they not only healed the wounds inflicted by infidelity but emerged with a love that had been tempered by fire—a love that could withstand the storms of life.

Their story serves as an inspiring reminder that even in the face of betrayal, redemption and renewal are possible. Stephen and Alyssa's journey demonstrates that love, when nurtured with patience, understanding, and an unwavering commitment, can conquer the darkest of shadows and emerge brighter and more resilient than ever before.

Chapter One

UNDERSTANDING INFIDELITY

Infidelity, a complex and sensitive topic, has been a subject of fascination and concern throughout human history. It refers to the act of engaging in a romantic or sexual relationship with someone outside of a committed partnership, betraying the trust and fidelity expected within that relationship. While infidelity is widely considered a breach of trust, its underlying causes and consequences vary greatly, making it an intriguing and nuanced phenomenon worthy of exploration.

To grasp the complexities of infidelity, one must consider its underlying motives. Human beings are intricate creatures driven by a range of emotions, desires, and needs. Relationships, by their very nature, require individuals to navigate the delicate balance between personal satisfaction and the commitment to their partner. Infidelity often emerges when this balance is disrupted, presenting an opportunity for exploration, escape, or a search for something lacking in the existing relationship.

One crucial aspect of understanding infidelity is recognizing that it is not a one-size-fits-all concept. The motives behind infidelity can differ significantly from person to person, and therefore, it is essential to avoid generalizations or oversimplifications. While some individuals may cheat due to dissatisfaction with their current relationship, others may seek novelty or excitement, struggle with impulse control, or succumb to the allure of forbidden experiences. Each case is unique, influenced by personal circumstances, psychological factors, and individual histories.

Psychological research offers valuable insights into the motivations behind infidelity. Some theories suggest that individuals engage in extramarital affairs as a means of meeting unmet emotional or sexual needs. For example, a person might seek emotional support or validation outside of their primary relationship if they feel neglected or unappreciated by their partner. Similarly, sexual dissatisfaction within a relationship can drive someone to seek fulfillment elsewhere.

Moreover, infidelity can also be seen as a response to personal vulnerabilities or unresolved issues. Individuals who struggle with low self-esteem, unresolved trauma, or a fear of intimacy may be more prone to seeking validation or escape through infidelity. These underlying psychological factors can create a fertile ground for betraying one's partner, as individuals attempt to fill emotional voids or avoid confronting their own internal struggles.

Societal and cultural factors also influence the prevalence and understanding of infidelity. While monogamy is often considered the norm in many cultures, different societies have diverse attitudes toward extramarital relationships. Some cultures may view infidelity as a severe transgression, whereas others may be more accepting or even condone certain forms of non-monogamous relationships.

Understanding the broader cultural context is crucial in comprehending the nuanced perspectives surrounding infidelity.

Furthermore, the advent of technology and the rise of social media have introduced new avenues for infidelity. The digital age has made it easier than ever to connect with others, fostering a sense of anonymity and providing opportunities for secretive interactions. Online platforms, dating apps, and social networking sites have expanded the possibilities for infidelity, blurring the boundaries between physical and virtual encounters. This digital landscape presents additional challenges for individuals navigating the complexities of trust and fidelity in their relationships.

The consequences of infidelity can be profound and far-reaching. Betrayal can shatter the foundation of trust within a relationship, leaving long-lasting emotional scars. The discovery of an affair often leads to feelings of shock, anger, and profound sadness. The repercussions extend beyond the immediate couple, impacting families, children, and social networks. Divorce rates have been shown to be higher among couples who have experienced infidelity, highlighting the profound disruption it can cause within the fabric of a relationship.

However, it is important to note that not all relationships end in separation or divorce after infidelity. Some couples choose to navigate the difficult path of healing and rebuilding trust, seeking therapy or counseling to address the underlying issues that led to the affair. These couples may find that the process of recovering from infidelity can be an opportunity for growth and introspection. It requires both partners to engage in open and honest communication, to confront the root causes of the affair, and to work towards rebuilding trust.

Rebuilding trust is a complex and delicate process. The partner who strayed must take responsibility for their actions and demonstrate sincere remorse. They must be willing to be transparent, allowing their partner to access their whereabouts, communication, and online activities, if necessary, as a means of rebuilding trust. The betrayed partner, on the other hand, faces the challenging task of forgiving and moving forward while also addressing their own feelings of hurt and betrayal.

Therapy can play a crucial role in this healing process. Couples therapy provides a safe space for both partners to express their emotions, fears, and concerns. A skilled therapist can guide the couple through difficult conversations, helping them explore the underlying dynamics of their relationship and the factors that contributed to the affair. Through therapy, couples can learn healthier communication patterns, develop strategies to rebuild trust, and establish new boundaries that foster a stronger and more resilient relationship.

It is worth noting that infidelity does not always indicate the end of a relationship.

Some couples may find that, in the aftermath of an affair, their relationship undergoes a transformation. The crisis can serve as a catalyst for growth, leading to a deeper understanding of each other's needs, desires, and vulnerabilities. In such cases, infidelity becomes a wake-up call that prompts both partners to reevaluate their commitment, rediscover their connection, and invest in the necessary changes to create a more fulfilling partnership.

However, it is essential to recognize that not all relationships can or should survive infidelity. Some couples may find that the damage caused by the affair is irreparable, and the pain and lack of trust are too significant to overcome. In these cases, the best course of action may be to part ways and seek individual healing and growth.

Understanding infidelity requires a nuanced approach that considers the intricate interplay of personal, psychological, cultural, and societal factors. It is crucial to avoid moral judgments and instead foster empathy and compassion when discussing and addressing infidelity. Recognizing the complexities of human nature and relationships allows for a more comprehensive understanding of infidelity and opens the door to meaningful conversations and interventions.

In conclusion, infidelity could arise from a variety of complex motives and circumstances. It challenges the notions of trust, commitment, and fidelity within relationships. While the consequences of infidelity can be profound and devastating, there is also the potential for growth, healing, and transformation. By approaching infidelity with empathy, understanding, and a commitment to open communication, individuals and couples can navigate this complex terrain and work towards building stronger and more fulfilling relationships.

Types of Infidelity

Infidelity is an age-old dilemma that has plagued human connections for centuries. It is a phenomenon, encompassing a wide range of behaviors and motivations. While the fundamental essence of infidelity remains the same—an act of disloyalty and breach of trust—the ways in which it manifests can be incredibly diverse. From physical encounters to emotional entanglements, infidelity is a complex web of betrayals, each with its own unique set of consequences. In this section, we delve into the various types of infidelity, shedding light on the intricacies that make them so deeply impactful.

Physical Infidelity

Physical infidelity is perhaps the most commonly recognized form of betrayal. It involves engaging in intimate acts with someone other than one's partner, thus breaching the exclusivity expected in a committed relationship. These acts can range from a single sexual encounter to sustained affairs that may continue over an extended period. Physical infidelity is often characterized by clandestine meetings, secret trysts, and a desire for sexual gratification outside the established partnership.

Emotional Infidelity

Unlike physical infidelity, emotional infidelity revolves around the development of deep emotional connections with someone other than a committed partner. This type of betrayal occurs when an individual forms a strong bond, confides in, and seeks emotional support from someone outside the primary relationship. Emotional infidelity may involve sharing intimate thoughts, desires, and aspirations with this third party, which can erode the emotional connection between partners and lead to a sense of emotional betrayal.

Cyber Infidelity

In today's technologically advanced world, a new form of infidelity has emerged—cyber infidelity. This type of betrayal occurs in the virtual realm, where individuals engage in explicit conversations, sexting, or exchange sexually explicit images/videos with someone other than their partner. Cyber infidelity can take place through social media platforms, dating apps, or online chat rooms. The ease of access and anonymity provided by the digital landscape has amplified the prevalence of cyber infidelity, making it a pressing concern for many couples.

Opportunistic Infidelity

Opportunistic infidelity stems from the occurrence of impulsive actions, often without any premeditation or emotional involvement. It happens when individuals find themselves in situations where the opportunity for a sexual or romantic encounter presents itself unexpectedly, and they succumb to temptation. Although opportunistic infidelity may not involve a strong emotional connection, it still represents a breach of trust and can cause significant distress to the betrayed partner.

Serial Infidelity

Serial infidelity is characterized by a repetitive pattern of betrayals, where an individual engages in multiple instances of unfaithful behavior with different partners. It goes beyond an isolated incident, indicating a deeper underlying issue within the individual's commitment to their relationship. Serial infidelity can be driven by a variety of factors, such as thrill-seeking, a lack of impulse control, or a constant search for novelty and excitement.

Narcissistic Infidelity

Narcissistic infidelity occurs when an individual engages in unfaithful behavior to bolster their own ego and self-esteem. These individuals seek validation and admiration from multiple sources, often using extramarital affairs as a means to feed their own inflated sense of self-importance. Narcissistic infidelity is not only a betrayal of trust but also a reflection of deep-rooted personality traits that can complicate the dynamics of a relationship further.

Revenge Infidelity

Revenge infidelity is a retaliatory act, born out of a desire to inflict pain or seek revenge on a partner who has previously been unfaithful. It is a response to the hurt and betrayal experienced by the aggrieved party, who, in an attempt to balance the scales, engages in their own act of infidelity. Revenge infidelity is a manifestation of deep emotional turmoil and can perpetuate a cycle of hurt and betrayal within the relationship. It often stems from a sense of anger, resentment, and a desire to regain a sense of power or control.

Financial Infidelity

Infidelity is not limited to matters of the heart or physical intimacy; it can also extend to the realm of finances. Financial infidelity occurs when one partner conceals or misuses money, assets, or incurs significant debt without the knowledge or consent of their partner. This form of betrayal erodes trust, disrupts financial stability, and can have long-lasting consequences for the relationship's overall well-being.

Imaginary Infidelity

In some cases, infidelity may not involve actual physical or emotional encounters but rather a preoccupation with an imaginary or fantasy world. Imaginary infidelity refers to situations where one partner becomes deeply engrossed in fantasies, idealized relationships, or even fictional characters, to the point where it disrupts their emotional connection and intimacy with their real-life partner. This form of infidelity can lead to feelings of neglect, dissatisfaction, and a lack of fulfillment within the relationship.

It is important to note that the impact and consequences of infidelity can vary greatly from one relationship to another. Each couple's unique dynamics, values, and communication patterns play a significant role in determining the severity of the betrayal and the potential for healing and reconciliation. Understanding the complexities of different types of infidelity can provide insights into the underlying issues within a relationship and help individuals navigate the challenges they face.

Ultimately, addressing infidelity requires open and honest communication, willingness to confront the issues at hand, and a commitment to rebuilding trust. Professional guidance, such as couples therapy, can also be instrumental in facilitating the healing process and providing a supportive environment for couples to explore the complexities of their relationship.

Infidelity, with its intricate web of motivations and repercussions, serves as a reminder of the fragility of trust within intimate connections. By recognizing and understanding the various types of infidelity, individuals can gain insights into the complex dynamics at play and work towards creating healthier, more fulfilling relationships based on transparency, respect, and mutual commitment.

Causes Of Infidelity

Infidelity can stem from a myriad of causes and motivations, which could unfortunately be used as justifications sometimes. How sad!

Understanding these underlying factors can shed light on the complexities that drive individuals to breach the boundaries of a committed relationship. While it is important to note that each situation is unique and context-dependent, there are several common causes and motivations that have been observed in cases of infidelity.

Δ Emotional Dissatisfaction

One of the primary causes of infidelity is emotional dissatisfaction within a relationship. When individuals feel unfulfilled emotionally, whether due to a lack of intimacy, poor communication, or unresolved conflicts, they may seek emotional connection and validation outside of the relationship. The allure of finding someone who understands and empathizes with their emotional needs can be a powerful motivator for seeking solace in an extramarital affair.

Δ Sexual Dissatisfaction

Sexual dissatisfaction can also play a significant role in driving individuals toward infidelity. When couples experience a decline in sexual desire, frequency, or compatibility, it can create a void that some individuals may try to fill through sexual encounters outside the relationship. The desire for novelty, excitement, or a specific sexual experience that is lacking within the primary relationship can lead individuals to seek satisfaction elsewhere.

Δ Lack of Commitment

A lack of commitment to the relationship can make individuals more susceptible to infidelity. This lack of commitment may stem from various factors such as fear of intimacy, commitment issues, or a belief that monogamy is not essential. When individuals do not prioritize the exclusivity and fidelity of the relationship, they may be more inclined to engage in extramarital affairs without considering the consequences.

Δ Desire for Novelty and Excitement

Human beings are naturally drawn to novelty and excitement, and these desires can sometimes lead to infidelity. The monotony and predictability that can arise in long-term relationships may trigger a craving for new experiences and the thrill of the forbidden. The pursuit of novelty can manifest in various ways, including seeking new romantic or sexual partners outside the committed relationship.

Δ Unmet Needs and Unrealistic Expectations

Unmet needs and unrealistic expectations within a relationship can create a breeding ground for infidelity. When individuals feel that their needs for love, attention, admiration, or validation are consistently unmet, they may be driven to seek fulfillment elsewhere. Similarly, unrealistic expectations of their partner or the relationship itself can set the stage for disappointment, which may prompt individuals to look for what they perceive as missing elsewhere.

Δ Emotional or Psychological Issues

Individuals grappling with emotional or psychological issues may be more susceptible to infidelity. Personal struggles such as low self-esteem, unresolved past trauma, or a need for external validation can contribute to seeking solace or escape through extramarital affairs. These underlying issues may temporarily alleviate emotional pain or provide a sense of control or empowerment.

Δ Opportunity and Circumstances

Opportunity and circumstances can also play a role in infidelity. When individuals find themselves in situations where there are ample opportunities for extramarital encounters, such as business trips, social gatherings, or online platforms, the temptation to engage in infidelity may become heightened. Factors such as proximity to potential partners, peer influence, or even alcohol or drug use can further increase the likelihood of succumbing to temptation.

Δ Revenge or Retaliation

In some cases, infidelity may be driven by a desire for revenge or retaliation. When an individual discovers or suspects their partner's infidelity, they may be driven to seek retribution by engaging in their own extramarital affair. This act of revenge is often rooted in a deep sense of hurt, anger, and a need to restore a sense of power or balance within the relationship.

Impact on the Betrayed Partner

Infidelity often has a profound and enduring impact on the betrayed partner. The emotional, psychological, and relational consequences of infidelity can be deeply distressing, reshaping the betrayed partner's life in ways that are both immediate and long-lasting. Understanding the complexities of these impacts is essential in navigating the painful aftermath and seeking avenues for healing and recovery.

Devastating Emotional Rollercoaster:
Discovering that one's partner has been unfaithful can trigger a devastating emotional rollercoaster for the betrayed partner. Shock, disbelief, anger, sadness, and profound hurt permeate their being, leaving them feeling emotionally shattered. The depth of the betrayal can generate a profound sense of grief and loss, as if mourning the death of the relationship they once knew and cherished.

Profound Sense of Betrayal:

Infidelity strikes at the core of trust within the relationship, leaving the betrayed partner with a profound sense of betrayal. The very foundation on which their relationship was built crumbles, leaving them questioning the authenticity of their partner's words, actions, and intentions. The breach of trust can result in feelings of deep hurt and resentment, eroding the sense of security and stability they once had.

Intense Self-Doubt and Insecurity:

The impact of infidelity often leads to intense self-doubt and insecurity in the betrayed partner. They may question their worthiness, attractiveness, and adequacy as a partner. Insecurities can emerge, fueled by comparisons with the person with whom their partner engaged in the affair. The betrayed partner may wonder what they lacked or how they failed, despite the knowledge that infidelity is not a reflection of their own shortcomings.

Sense of Shame and Embarrassment:

The discovery of infidelity can evoke a lingering sense of shame and embarrassment in the betrayed partner. They may grapple with feelings of being humiliated, especially when faced with the judgment and opinions of others. The fear of being stigmatized or blamed can exacerbate the emotional burden, potentially hindering their ability to seek support or share their experiences with others.

Trust Issues and Fear of Future Betrayal:
Infidelity leaves an indelible mark on the betrayed partner's ability to trust again. The betrayal serves as a painful reminder that trust can be broken, leading to a heightened sense of vigilance and skepticism in future relationships. Trust issues can permeate subsequent connections, making it challenging to fully open up and establish the same level of vulnerability and intimacy.

Emotional Scars and Post-Traumatic Stress:

The impact of infidelity can result in emotional scars that endure long after the initial shock subsides. The betrayed partner may experience symptoms akin to post-traumatic stress disorder (PTSD), such as intrusive thoughts, flashbacks, or nightmares related to the infidelity. The trauma of the betrayal can persist, affecting their overall emotional well-being and future relationships.

Impact on Self-Esteem and Identity:

Infidelity can have a profound impact on the betrayed partner's self-esteem and self-identity. The betrayal can lead to a diminished sense of self-worth, as the betrayed partner may internalize the belief that they were not enough to satisfy their partner's needs. They may struggle with feelings of inadequacy, questioning their desirability and value as a person.

Emotional Withdrawal and Fear of Vulnerability:

As a result of the betrayal, the betrayed partner may withdraw emotionally as a protective mechanism. The fear of being hurt again can make them hesitant to express their emotions or engage in vulnerable connections. The emotional withdrawal can strain the relationship and hinder the possibility of rebuilding trust and intimacy. The betrayed partner may build emotional walls, fearing that vulnerability will only lead to further pain and betrayal.

Impact on Mental Health:

Infidelity can take a toll on the betrayed partner's mental health. The emotional upheaval, constant rumination, and distress caused by the betrayal can contribute to the development or exacerbation of conditions such as anxiety and depression. The profound sense of loss and shattered trust can leave them feeling overwhelmed and struggling to regain a sense of emotional stability.

Difficulty in Forgiveness and Healing:
Forgiveness is a complex process that the betrayed partner may struggle with. The journey toward forgiveness is often lengthy and challenging, requiring a deep exploration of emotions, understanding, and a willingness to let go of the pain. The act of forgiving does not imply forgetting or condoning infidelity but rather an opportunity to find peace and release the grip of bitterness and resentment. Forgiveness here, is basically the ability to remember without being so pained.

Impact on Future Relationships:
The impact of infidelity extends beyond the boundaries of the current relationship and can influence future connections. The betrayed partner may approach future relationships with caution, fearing a repetition of the pain they experienced. They may be hesitant to fully trust and invest emotionally, guarding themselves against potential betrayal. Navigating future relationships requires careful self-reflection and self-care; and an understanding that

not all relationships will follow the same path as the one marred by infidelity.

Opportunity for Personal Growth and Transformation:

While the impact of infidelity is undoubtedly devastating, it can also serve as an opportunity for personal growth and transformation. The betrayed partner may embark on a journey of self-discovery, reassessing their own needs, boundaries, and values. They may seek therapy or counseling to process their emotions, heal from the betrayal, and develop a stronger sense of self. Through self-reflection and growth, they can emerge from the experience with newfound resilience, wisdom, and the ability to create healthier relationships in the future. The bright side, right?

Chapter Two

COPING WITH BETRAYAL

Discovering that your partner has been unfaithful is a devastating and life-altering experience. The pain, betrayal, and emotional turmoil that accompany infidelity can be overwhelming, leaving you unsure of how to move forward. Coping with infidelity is a complex and individualized process, as each person's response and needs are unique. However, there are certain strategies and approaches that can help navigate this difficult journey of healing and recovery.

Δ Allow Yourself to Feel the Emotions:
When faced with infidelity, it is natural to experience a range of intense emotions. Allow yourself to feel them fully without judgment or self-restraint. Anger, sadness, betrayal, confusion, and even relief are all valid emotional responses. Acknowledge and honor these emotions, as they are an essential part of the healing process.

Δ Seek Support from Trusted Individuals:
Reaching out for support during this challenging time is crucial. Share your experience with close friends, family members, or a therapist who can provide a safe and non-judgmental space for you to express your feelings and thoughts. Surrounding yourself with a support network can offer comfort, validation, and guidance as you navigate the journey of coping with infidelity.

Δ Prioritize Self-Care:
Taking care of your physical, emotional, and mental well-being is vital when coping with infidelity. Engage in activities that bring you joy, relaxation, and comfort. Practice self-compassion and be gentle with yourself as you heal. This may involve exercise, mindfulness practices, engaging in hobbies, or seeking professional help when needed.

Δ Understand That Healing Takes Time:
Recovering from the impact of infidelity is a process that cannot be rushed. It takes time to heal emotional wounds and rebuild trust.

Be patient with yourself and allow the healing journey to unfold naturally. Remember that healing is not linear, and there may be setbacks along the way. Progress may be gradual, but with time, the intensity of emotions will subside, and healing will occur.

Δ Engage in Open and Honest Communication:
Effective communication is essential when coping with infidelity. Establish an open and honest dialogue with your partner, allowing for a safe space to express your feelings, concerns, and needs. This may involve difficult conversations about the infidelity, exploring the underlying issues in the relationship, and discussing ways to rebuild trust. A skilled couples therapist can facilitate these conversations and help navigate the process of rebuilding the relationship if both partners are willing.

Δ Set Clear Boundaries and Expectations:
Establishing clear boundaries and expectations is crucial when working through the aftermath of infidelity. Define

what is acceptable and unacceptable behavior moving forward. Communicate your needs and boundaries to your partner and be willing to listen to theirs. Setting clear boundaries provides a sense of security and helps rebuild trust as both partners navigate the path to healing.

Δ Consider Seeking Professional Help:
Coping with infidelity can be an incredibly challenging and complex process. Professional help, such as individual therapy or couples counseling, can provide invaluable guidance and support. A skilled therapist can help you navigate the emotions, facilitate communication, and assist in rebuilding trust and intimacy. Therapy can also help address underlying issues within the relationship that may have contributed to the infidelity.

Δ Practice Self-Reflection and Acceptance:
Engage in self-reflection to gain insight into your own needs, desires, and contributions to the relationship. This introspective process allows for personal growth and can help you make informed decisions about

the future of the relationship. Acceptance is also a key aspect of coping with infidelity. While this does not mean condoning betrayal, acceptance in this context involves acknowledging the reality of the situation and finding a way to move forward, with or without the "betrayer".

Initial Reactions and Emotional Turmoil

The initial discovery of an unfaithful partner can send shockwaves through one's entire being, eliciting a wide range of intense and conflicting emotions. It is an emotional turmoil that engulfs the wounded party, leaving them bewildered, heartbroken, and questioning everything they once believed to be true.

At first, the revelation may trigger a surge of disbelief, as if reality has been momentarily suspended. The mind struggles to reconcile the evidence with the image of the partner they thought they knew, desperately searching for alternative explanations, hoping against hope that there has been a grave misunderstanding. The heart, however, is not easily swayed, and as the undeniable truth seeps in, disbelief gives way to a profound sense of betrayal.

Betrayal, that treacherous companion, consumes the injured soul. Waves of anger crash against the shores of reason, threatening to drown out all other emotions. The unfaithful partner's actions become an affront to trust, a violation of the sacred bond that was meant to be inviolable. The betrayed one feels not only deceived, but also robbed of their sense of security and stability. Doubts, once buried deep within, rise to the surface, casting a shadow over every shared memory and affectionate gesture.

Grief takes hold, wrapping its sorrowful tendrils around the heart. It is a mourning of the relationship that once held promise and warmth, now tainted by infidelity. The pain is both immediate and lingering, an ache that permeates every aspect of life. Sleep becomes elusive, replaced by nights spent replaying the painful discovery and the subsequent unraveling of trust. Appetites diminish as the heaviness in the chest suppresses the hunger for sustenance, leaving a hollow emptiness in its wake.

Simultaneously, a storm of self-doubt brews within. Questions haunt the wounded soul: "What did I do wrong? Was I not enough?"

Insecurities, often dormant, resurface with a vengeance, amplifying the already overwhelming emotional distress. The betrayed partner may question their own worth, feeling inadequate and undeserving of love. Confidence wanes, replaced by self-blame and a deep-seated fear of being unlovable.

Amidst the chaos of emotions, there may also be glimpses of resentment. The unfaithful partner becomes the target of anger, their actions deemed unforgivable. The wounded soul yearns for retribution, a desire to inflict upon the perpetrator the same pain they have endured. These vengeful thoughts, though understandable in the face of such emotional devastation, can further entangle the heart in bitterness, hindering the healing process.

Yet, through the tempest of emotions, there may also be moments of clarity. The betrayed partner begins to recognize their own strength and resilience, slowly emerging from the depths of despair. With time, forgiveness becomes a possibility, although a distant one. It requires a journey of self-discovery and introspection, where boundaries are reestablished, wounds are mended, and the shattered pieces of trust are painstakingly reconstructed.

The initial reaction and emotional turmoil that accompany the discovery of an unfaithful partner are undeniably overwhelming. It is a chaotic symphony of disbelief, betrayal, grief, self-doubt, and resentment. The wounded soul must navigate this tumultuous landscape, acknowledging and processing each emotion as it arises, in order to find solace, healing, and ultimately, the strength to move forward.

Blame and Accountability

When an individual acknowledges their infidelity and embarks on the path to recovery, they must confront the weighty concepts of blame and accountability. These two intertwined elements play a pivotal role in the healing process, demanding a complex and nuanced understanding of one's actions and their consequences. It is through the lens of blame and accountability that the unfaithful partner can begin to rebuild trust, seek forgiveness, and ultimately strive for personal growth.

Blame, in the context of infidelity, can be a double-edged sword. Initially, it is natural for the betrayed partner to assign blame to the unfaithful one, viewing their actions as the sole catalyst for the pain and turmoil that has ensued. This blame becomes a shield, protecting the wounded heart from fully accepting the harsh reality of betrayal. However, the unfaithful partner must resist the temptation to deflect or deny responsibility, acknowledging their role in the breach of trust.

Accepting blame is not an easy feat. It requires a profound level of introspection and humility. The unfaithful partner must confront their own actions and motivations, recognizing the choices they made that led them down the path of infidelity. It demands an honest examination of the vulnerabilities, insecurities, or dissatisfaction within themselves or the relationship that contributed to their betrayal. This process, while painful, is essential for personal growth and a sincere commitment to change.

Yet, blame should not be a stagnant entity. **It must evolve into accountability**—a dynamic force that propels the unfaithful partner forward. Accountability is the willingness to face the consequences of one's actions, to actively participate in the healing process, and to make amends. It involves taking ownership of the pain caused, without shifting the burden entirely onto the betrayed partner.

Accountability requires the unfaithful partner to demonstrate a deep understanding of the profound impact of their actions on their partner's emotional well-being. It entails empathizing with the hurt and acknowledging the long-lasting scars that infidelity can inflict. This empathy, coupled with genuine remorse, becomes the driving force behind meaningful actions and efforts towards rebuilding trust.

Transparency becomes paramount in the quest for accountability. The unfaithful partner must be willing to lay bare the details of their infidelity, answering the betrayed partner's questions honestly and openly. It is through this vulnerability that the betrayed partner can begin to grasp the full extent of the betrayal and find solace in the unfaithful partner's unwavering commitment to honesty. Transparency also involves relinquishing any secrecy or deceit, allowing for a clean slate upon which trust can gradually be rebuilt.

Accountability extends beyond mere words and promises. It necessitates consistent and tangible efforts to make amends and to address the underlying issues that led to the infidelity. The unfaithful partner must actively engage in self-reflection and seek professional help if necessary, to understand the root causes of their actions and to develop healthier coping mechanisms. This process may involve therapy, counseling, or participation in support groups dedicated to relationship recovery.

While blame and accountability primarily focus on the unfaithful partner's actions, it is important to acknowledge that healing is a shared responsibility. The betrayed partner must also be open to the possibility of forgiveness and engage in their own emotional journey. The unfaithful partner must respect this process, offering unwavering support and understanding as the betrayed partner grapples with their own feelings of hurt, anger, and distrust.

Ultimately, blame and accountability are essential components of the recovery process for an unfaithful partner. By accepting blame, embracing accountability, and actively working towards personal growth and relationship repair, the unfaithful partner can foster an environment of healing, rebuild trust, and strive for a future founded on honesty, empathy, and mutual respect.

If You Cheated

When confronted with the challenging aftermath of infidelity, both the individual who cheated and the one who was cheated on face distinct paths towards healing and rebuilding their relationship. Each role requires unique considerations, actions, and commitments to make the relationship work again. Let us delve into the steps one can take in each scenario, outlining a roadmap towards reconciliation and renewed trust.

For the individual who cheated, self-reflection becomes paramount. It is crucial to examine the motivations, vulnerabilities, and insecurities that contributed to the betrayal. Taking responsibility for one's actions is the first step towards repairing the damage caused. Here are several key actions to consider:

Acknowledge and end the affair: The first and foremost step is to terminate the extramarital relationship or affair completely. This demonstrates a genuine commitment to repairing the primary relationship and allows space for introspection.

Reflect on motivations and seek therapy: Engaging in self-reflection is vital to understand why the infidelity occurred. Seeking the guidance of a qualified therapist or counselor can provide valuable insights into underlying issues, such as personal insecurities, communication breakdowns, or unmet needs within the relationship. Therapy can also aid in developing healthier coping mechanisms and improving emotional intelligence.

Communicate openly and honestly: Transparent communication is essential for rebuilding trust. The individual who cheated should be prepared to answer their partner's questions openly and honestly, providing the betrayed partner with the necessary information for closure and understanding. It is important to remember that healing takes time and patience, and the betrayed partner may need to revisit their questions and concerns throughout the process.

Express genuine remorse and apologize: Genuine remorse is a vital component of rebuilding trust. The individual who cheated must express sincere regret for their actions, taking responsibility for the pain they caused. A heartfelt apology that acknowledges the hurt, demonstrates empathy, and conveys a commitment to change can lay the foundation for reconciliation.

Rebuild trust through transparency and consistency: Trust is a fragile entity that requires time and consistent effort to rebuild. The individual who cheated must be transparent in their actions, allowing their partner access to their whereabouts, communication, and other areas that may have been compromised during the affair. By consistently demonstrating your trustworthiness, honoring commitments, and being accountable, trust can be gradually restored.

Show patience and understanding: The healing process for the betrayed partner may be long and challenging. It is crucial for the individual who cheated to show patience, understanding, and empathy throughout this journey. This includes providing emotional support, actively listening to the betrayed partner's concerns, and being willing to make amends whenever necessary.

If You Were Cheated On

For the individual who was cheated on, the path to healing requires confronting and processing the emotions associated with betrayal. Rebuilding trust may seem daunting, but with commitment and open communication, it is possible to restore the relationship. Here are some steps to consider:

Allow yourself to feel and process emotions: The discovery of infidelity can trigger a range of intense emotions such as anger, hurt, and betrayal. It is important to acknowledge these feelings, allowing yourself time and space to process them. Seek support from trusted friends, family, or a therapist who can provide guidance and help navigate through the emotional turmoil.

Establish clear boundaries and expectations: During the healing process, it is essential to establish clear boundaries and expectations with your partner. Open and honest communication is key. Discuss your needs, concerns, and fears, and work together to define the boundaries that will help rebuild trust. This may include increased transparency, setting limits on contact with the affair partner, or establishing new relationship dynamics.

Seek professional support: Individual therapy can be immensely beneficial in processing the emotional aftermath of infidelity. A qualified therapist can provide guidance, offer tools for effective communication, and help you navigate the complex emotions that arise during the healing process. Couples therapy may also be beneficial to facilitate open dialogue, enhance understanding, and rebuild the foundation of the relationship.

Determine the willingness to forgive: Forgiveness is a personal and individual decision that may take time. Consider whether forgiveness is a possibility for you and whether you are willing to work towards it. Forgiveness does not mean forgetting or condoning the betrayal but rather letting go of the resentment and anger to allow space for healing and growth.

Gradually rebuild trust: Rebuilding trust is a gradual process that requires consistent effort from both partners. The individual who was cheated on should communicate their needs for transparency and honesty, and the unfaithful partner should demonstrate their commitment to change. Over time, trust can be rebuilt through open communication, shared experiences, and consistent follow-through on commitments.

Practice self-care and self-reflection: It is crucial for the betrayed partner to prioritize self-care and engage in self-reflection throughout the healing process. This includes practicing self-compassion, engaging in activities that bring joy and fulfillment, and taking the time to understand personal boundaries, needs, and desires within the relationship.

Bottomline: Both the individual who cheated and the one who was cheated on must approach the healing process with patience, empathy, and a genuine desire to rebuild the relationship. It is an intricate journey that requires open communication, self-reflection, therapy, and a commitment to personal growth. By taking the necessary steps and fostering understanding, it is possible to mend the shattered trust and create a stronger, more resilient partnership.

Chapter Three

REBUILDING TRUST

Rebuilding trust after infidelity is an exhausting but necessary stride towards the destination of recovery. It requires a delicate balance of patience, understanding, and consistent effort from both the unfaithful partner and the betrayed one. Trust, once shattered, cannot be mended overnight. It demands a comprehensive approach that encompasses transparency, open communication, and a steadfast commitment to rebuilding the foundation of the relationship.

The process of rebuilding trust begins with acknowledging the magnitude of the betrayal. The unfaithful partner must fully grasp the depth of the pain and damage caused by their actions. It is essential for them to take responsibility, expressing genuine remorse and acknowledging the hurt they have inflicted upon their partner.

Transparency becomes a cornerstone in the quest for rebuilding trust. The unfaithful partner must be willing to open themselves up, allowing their actions and intentions to be scrutinized. This includes sharing information willingly, being forthcoming about their whereabouts, and making a conscious effort to rebuild a sense of security and predictability within the relationship.

Open communication plays a vital role in rebuilding trust. The unfaithful partner should be receptive to their partner's feelings, concerns, and questions. It is crucial to create an environment where the betrayed partner feels safe to express their emotions without fear of judgment or retaliation. Active listening, empathy, and validating their emotions can foster a sense of understanding and begin to rebuild the emotional connection that was severed by the infidelity.

Consistency is key in the process of rebuilding trust. The unfaithful partner must demonstrate a consistent pattern of trustworthy behavior over time. This involves following through on commitments, being accountable for their actions, and showing up consistently for their partner. Small gestures of reliability and dependability can gradually rebuild trust, demonstrating a genuine change in behavior.

Patience is a virtue in the journey of rebuilding trust. Healing takes time, and the betrayed partner may experience moments of doubt, insecurity, and vulnerability. The unfaithful partner must be patient, understanding that trust is not rebuilt overnight. It requires a consistent effort to rebuild the emotional bond and a willingness to support the betrayed partner throughout their healing process.

Rebuilding trust also involves addressing the underlying issues that led to the infidelity. The unfaithful partner should be willing to explore the root causes of their actions, such as personal vulnerabilities, unmet needs, or communication breakdowns within the relationship. This may involve individual therapy or couples counseling to identify and address these underlying issues, fostering personal growth and strengthening the foundation of the relationship.

Forgiveness is a crucial component of rebuilding trust, but it cannot be forced or rushed. The betrayed partner needs time to heal and process their emotions. Forgiveness should not be seen as a prerequisite for rebuilding trust, but rather as a potential outcome of the healing journey. It is a personal decision that may require time, introspection, and a genuine sense of remorse from the unfaithful partner.

Building trust after infidelity requires a willingness to let go of the past and embrace a new chapter in the relationship. Both partners must be committed to learning from the past, creating healthier relationship dynamics, and consciously working towards rebuilding trust. It is a joint effort that requires vulnerability, forgiveness, and a shared vision for the future.

Throughout this process, it is important to acknowledge that rebuilding trust does not guarantee the complete restoration of the relationship to its previous state. The relationship may be forever changed by the deed, and both partners must be willing to accept and navigate these changes. With time, effort, and a genuine commitment to growth and understanding, it is possible to rebuild trust and forge a new path towards a stronger, more resilient relationship.

The Place of Trust

Trust is the bedrock upon which a healthy and thriving relationship is built. It serves as the foundation of emotional intimacy, vulnerability, and mutual respect. However, when trust is shattered due to infidelity, the road to recovery becomes an intricate and challenging journey. Rebuilding trust is not only crucial for the survival of the relationship but also for the emotional well-being of both the betrayed partner and the unfaithful one. Let us explore the profound importance of trust in the process of recovery after infidelity.

Trust is the cornerstone of emotional safety within a relationship. It creates a sense of security and predictability, allowing both partners to be vulnerable and authentic. When infidelity occurs, this sense of safety is severely compromised, leaving the betrayed partner questioning the authenticity of their partner's words and actions. Restoring trust becomes paramount in order to create a space where both partners can feel secure and emotionally connected once again.

Rebuilding trust is not solely about regaining confidence in the unfaithful partner's fidelity. It goes beyond mere faithfulness; it encompasses honesty, transparency, and reliability in all aspects of the relationship. Trust requires consistency and dependability in words and actions, forming the building blocks of a secure and stable partnership.

Infidelity disrupts the trust that has been carefully cultivated over time. It shatters the belief in the unfaithful partner's commitment, honesty, and integrity. Thus, the journey of recovery must include a deep and genuine understanding of the pain and damage caused by the betrayal. The unfaithful partner must fully grasp the gravity of their actions and the profound impact it has had on their partner's trust.

Rebuilding trust requires open and honest communication. The betrayed partner needs space to express their emotions, concerns, and fears. They must be given the opportunity to voice their doubts and ask questions in order to gain clarity and closure. The unfaithful partner, in turn, must be receptive and willing to engage in these conversations, listening actively and demonstrating empathy. This open dialogue fosters understanding and paves the way for the rebuilding of trust.

Transparency is a crucial component of rebuilding trust after infidelity. The unfaithful partner must be willing to be transparent and open in all aspects of their lives. This may involve sharing their whereabouts, allowing access to communication devices, and providing a clear understanding of their actions and intentions. Transparency creates a sense of accountability and helps bridge the gap created by the breach of trust.

Consistency is paramount in the journey of rebuilding trust. Words and actions must align consistently over time. The unfaithful partner must demonstrate a consistent pattern of trustworthy behavior, following through on commitments and being accountable for their actions. It is through consistent and reliable behavior that trust is gradually restored, fostering a renewed belief in the unfaithful partner's integrity.

Patience is an essential virtue in the process of rebuilding trust. Healing from the pain of infidelity takes time, and the betrayed partner may experience moments of doubt and insecurity. The unfaithful partner must be patient, understanding that trust cannot be rebuilt overnight. It requires a consistent effort to rebuild the emotional connection and a willingness to support the betrayed partner throughout their healing process.

Rebuilding trust after infidelity also necessitates addressing the underlying issues that led to the betrayal. Both partners must be willing to confront and explore the root causes of the infidelity. This may involve individual therapy or couples counseling to delve into personal vulnerabilities, unmet needs, or communication breakdowns within the relationship. By addressing these underlying issues, the couple can work towards personal growth and create a healthier and more resilient relationship.

Forgiveness plays a pivotal role in the process of rebuilding trust. It is a complex and deeply personal decision that requires time, introspection, and a genuine sense of remorse from the unfaithful partner.

Forgiveness should not be viewed as an obligation but as a potential outcome of the healing journey.

It involves letting go of the resentment and anger, allowing space for healing and growth. Forgiveness does not mean forgetting or condoning the deed (infidelity) but rather opening up to the possibility of rebuilding trust and creating a new future together.

The importance of trust in the recovery process after infidelity cannot be overstated. Without trust, the relationship remains fragile, plagued by doubt, and lacking emotional intimacy. Trust is the thread that weaves together the intricate fabric of a healthy and fulfilling partnership. It requires commitment, vulnerability, and consistent effort from both partners. By rebuilding trust, couples can create a stronger and more resilient bond, capable of withstanding future challenges and fostering a deeper level of emotional connection.

Open and Honest Communication

Open and honest communication is an essential requirement for the process of recovery after infidelity. When trust is shattered, the foundation of a relationship is severely compromised, leaving both the betrayed partner and the unfaithful one in a state of emotional turmoil. Rebuilding trust requires a commitment to open and honest communication, as it is through these channels that understanding, healing, and ultimately, the restoration of the relationship can occur.

In the aftermath of infidelity, emotions run high and tensions are palpable. It is during this time that open and honest communication becomes paramount. The betrayed partner needs the space to express their feelings, concerns, and pain without fear of judgment or retaliation. They must be given the opportunity to articulate their emotions and seek answers to the questions that haunt them. By providing a safe and supportive environment for these conversations, the healing process can begin.

The unfaithful partner, too, must be willing to engage in open and honest communication. This requires a genuine willingness to listen, empathize, and take responsibility for their actions. They must be prepared to confront the difficult questions posed by their betrayed partner and provide the necessary information for understanding and closure. It is through this transparency that trust can begin to be rebuilt.

Open communication goes beyond discussing the immediate aftermath of the infidelity. It involves an ongoing dialogue about the impact of the betrayal, the needs of both partners, and the steps necessary to move forward. Both individuals must be willing to express their emotions, fears, and desires openly and honestly. This includes discussing their expectations for the future, setting boundaries, and addressing any lingering doubts or concerns.

However, open communication does not mean unrestricted disclosure of every detail. It is essential to strike a balance between transparency and respect for personal boundaries. The unfaithful partner should be mindful of the betrayed partner's emotional well-being and consider their readiness to receive certain information. Open communication should be guided by a shared understanding of what is necessary for healing and rebuilding trust.

Active listening is a crucial aspect of open and honest communication. Both partners must be present, attentive, and willing to truly hear each other's perspectives. This involves giving undivided attention, refraining from interrupting, and validating the emotions expressed. By actively listening, a safe space is created for the betrayed partner to share their pain and for the unfaithful partner to gain a deeper understanding of the impact of their actions.

Alongside active listening, empathy plays a vital role in open and honest communication. Empathy allows both partners to step into each other's shoes, to grasp the emotional turmoil experienced by the betrayed partner and the remorse felt by the unfaithful one. It involves seeking to understand the emotions underlying the words spoken and responding with compassion and understanding. By cultivating empathy, a bridge is built between the two individuals, fostering a sense of connection and facilitating the healing process.

Open and honest communication also requires the courage to address difficult topics and confront uncomfortable truths. Both partners must be willing to acknowledge their own shortcomings and vulnerabilities within the relationship. This may involve discussing underlying issues that contributed to the infidelity, such as a breakdown in communication, unmet needs, or unresolved conflicts. By confronting these issues openly, couples can work towards resolving them, ultimately strengthening the foundation of their relationship.

Professional guidance, such as couples therapy or individual counseling, can be invaluable in facilitating open and honest communication. A skilled therapist can provide a safe and structured environment for discussions, offer tools for effective communication, and guide the couple towards understanding and resolution. Therapy can also help identify patterns of communication that may have contributed to the breakdown of trust, empowering the couple to develop healthier and more effective communication strategies.

Rebuilding trust after infidelity is a complex and challenging process. It requires a deep commitment to open and honest communication from both partners. Through active listening, empathy, and willingness to address difficult topics, couples can lay the groundwork for understanding, healing, and ultimately, the restoration of trust. Open communication becomes the bridge that connects the hearts and minds of the betrayed partner and the unfaithful one, paving the way for a stronger relationship.

Demonstrating Consistency and Transparency

The demonstration of transparency and consistency is a vital requirement in the journey of recovery after infidelity. When trust has been shattered, rebuilding it becomes a delicate and intricate process that demands unwavering commitment from both the betrayed partner and the unfaithful one. Transparency and consistency serve as pillars of reassurance, helping to rebuild trust and create a solid foundation for the healing of the relationship.

Transparency is an essential component of rebuilding trust. It involves being open, honest, and forthcoming in all aspects of the relationship. The unfaithful partner must be willing to share information willingly, without hesitation or defensiveness. This may include providing details about their actions, their whereabouts, and any interactions that might raise concerns for their partner. Transparency allows the betrayed partner to gain a clearer understanding of the truth, helping to dispel doubt and rebuild a sense of security.

Consistency is equally crucial in the recovery process. It requires the unfaithful partner to demonstrate a consistent pattern of trustworthy behavior over time. Words and actions must align harmoniously, reflecting a genuine commitment to change and a dedication to rebuilding trust. Consistency means following through on commitments, honoring promises, and being reliable and dependable in the relationship. It is through consistent actions that the betrayed partner can begin to believe in the unfaithful partner's sincerity and integrity.

The unfaithful partner must recognize that transparency and consistency go hand in hand. It is not enough to share information sporadically or inconsistently. Rather, it requires a genuine willingness to be open and forthcoming at all times. Transparency should not be seen as a burden or an invasion of privacy, but rather as a necessary step towards rebuilding trust. By embracing transparency, the unfaithful partner demonstrates a commitment to healing and a desire to regain their partner's trust.

Consistency, on the other hand, requires the unfaithful partner to maintain a steadfast commitment to change. It means consistently adhering to the boundaries and agreements set within the relationship. This includes being punctual, reliable, and accountable for their actions. Consistency allows the betrayed partner to gradually regain confidence in the unfaithful partner's ability to uphold their commitments, ultimately rebuilding trust in their reliability and dependability.

Consistency and transparency are not achieved overnight. They require patience, understanding, and a genuine willingness to work towards rebuilding trust. The unfaithful partner must be prepared for setbacks and challenges along the way. It is normal for the betrayed partner to have moments of doubt and skepticism.

However, by consistently demonstrating transparency and maintaining a pattern of trustworthy behavior, the unfaithful partner can reassure their partner that they are committed to change and rebuilding the relationship.

It is important to note that demonstrating transparency and consistency is not a one-time effort. It is an ongoing commitment that must be nurtured and maintained throughout the healing process. The unfaithful partner must continuously communicate openly, share information willingly, and engage in honest conversations with their partner. By doing so, they create an environment where trust can flourish and the wounds of infidelity can slowly heal.

Consistency is not about perfection but rather about showing up and putting in the effort consistently. It means acknowledging mistakes and taking responsibility for them. If the unfaithful partner stumbles or makes a misstep, it is crucial for them to acknowledge their actions, apologize sincerely, and work to make amends. By demonstrating a consistent commitment to growth and change, the unfaithful partner can rebuild trust in their willingness to learn from their mistakes and improve themselves.

Transparency and consistency also require vulnerability. The unfaithful partner must be willing to share their emotions, thoughts, and fears openly. This vulnerability fosters a sense of connection and allows the betrayed partner to see the unfaithful partner's genuine remorse and desire for change. It is through vulnerability that true healing can occur, as both partners become more attuned to each other's needs and emotions.

In the process of recovery after infidelity, demonstrating transparency and consistency serves as a guiding light. These qualities provide reassurance, foster understanding, and create a sense of security within the relationship. By embracing transparency and consistency, couples can embark on a journey of healing, rebuilding trust, and forging an even more resilient bond.

Chapter Four

RESTORING INTIMACY

Granted, Infidelity is a painful breach of trust that can leave a lasting impact on a relationship. When one partner strays, it shatters the foundation of trust and undermines the intimate connection that once existed between them. However, if both partners are committed to healing and rebuilding the relationship, restoring intimacy becomes a vital requirement for recovery.

Intimacy is not limited to physical closeness; it encompasses emotional, intellectual, and spiritual aspects as well. After infidelity, all of these dimensions are profoundly affected, and rebuilding them requires a multifaceted approach. The journey toward restoring intimacy is a challenging one, but it is not impossible with sincere efforts and effective communication.

First and foremost, rebuilding trust is paramount in restoring intimacy. Trust, once broken, takes time and consistent actions to rebuild. The unfaithful partner must demonstrate remorse, take responsibility for their actions, and be transparent in their behavior. They need to willingly open themselves up to scrutiny and answer any questions their betrayed partner may have. By doing so, they lay the foundation for trust to be gradually reestablished.

Rebuilding trust also requires establishing new boundaries and agreements within the relationship. Both partners need to redefine their expectations and discuss what is acceptable to them moving forward. This renegotiation of boundaries allows them to regain a sense of security and reestablish a framework for the relationship. It requires open and honest communication, active listening, and a willingness to compromise.

In addition to trust, emotional intimacy must also be nurtured to restore the connection between partners. After infidelity, the betrayed partner may feel emotionally distant and guarded. They may be plagued by insecurities and fear of being hurt again. It is crucial for both partners to create a safe space where emotions can be expressed without judgment or defensiveness.

The betrayed partner needs reassurance that their feelings are valid and that their pain is acknowledged. The unfaithful partner must show empathy and compassion, actively listening to their partner's emotional needs and validating their experience. This process requires patience, understanding, and a willingness to confront and address difficult emotions.

Rebuilding emotional intimacy also entails rebuilding the friendship and companionship that may have been eroded by infidelity. Engaging in activities together, sharing hobbies, and spending quality time can help foster a sense of connection and closeness. By consciously investing in the friendship aspect of their relationship, the couple can rebuild a strong foundation upon which to rebuild their romantic bond.

Intellectual intimacy, often overlooked, is another crucial aspect of restoring the relationship after infidelity. Intellectual intimacy involves sharing thoughts, ideas, and engaging in stimulating conversations. It is a way for partners to connect on a deeper level and understand each other's values, beliefs, and aspirations. Engaging in intellectual discussions, exploring common interests, and seeking out new experiences together can help reignite this dimension of intimacy.

Lastly, **spiritual intimacy, if relevant to the couple, can play a vital role in the healing process.** This dimension involves sharing spiritual beliefs, engaging in shared practices, and seeking meaning and purpose together. For couples who find solace in their spiritual connection, integrating this dimension into their recovery journey can provide a source of strength, forgiveness, and renewal.

Restoring intimacy after infidelity is a complex and intricate process. It requires a deep commitment from both partners to work through the pain, rebuild trust, and create a new foundation for their relationship. Each partner must be willing to examine their own role in the breakdown and be open to growth and change.

Patience, understanding, and forgiveness are essential ingredients in this process. Healing takes time, and setbacks are to be expected along the way. It is crucial for both partners to practice self-compassion and extend empathy to one another. Professional guidance from a therapist who specializes in couples therapy can also provide invaluable support and guidance throughout the journey of restoring intimacy.

A skilled therapist can help the couple navigate the complex emotions, facilitate open communication, and provide tools and techniques to rebuild trust and intimacy. They can assist in identifying and addressing underlying issues that may have contributed to the infidelity, such as unresolved conflicts, unmet needs, or issues with self-esteem. With the guidance of a therapist, the couple can learn healthier ways of relating to each other and develop strategies to prevent future breaches of trust.

It is important to note that restoring intimacy does not mean erasing the memory of the infidelity. The betrayed partner may experience triggers and moments of insecurity even after significant progress has been made. Both partners must be willing to acknowledge and address these moments with compassion and understanding. By openly discussing their fears and concerns, the couple can strengthen their bond and deepen their understanding of each other.

As the process unfolds, the couple may discover that the restored intimacy surpasses the level they had before the infidelity occurred. The shared experiences, open communication, and the journey of healing can lead to a deeper connection and a more profound understanding of one another. This newfound intimacy can become a source of resilience and strength for the relationship moving forward.

It is essential to recognize that not all relationships can or should be restored after infidelity. In some cases, the damage may be irreparable, or one or both partners may not be willing or able to put in the necessary effort to rebuild trust and intimacy. In such situations, it may be healthier for both individuals to consider parting ways and pursuing individual healing.

However, for couples who are committed to the process and willing to invest in rebuilding their relationship, restoring intimacy is a vital requirement for recovery after infidelity. It involves rebuilding trust, nurturing emotional, intellectual, and spiritual connections, and seeking professional guidance when needed. It is a challenging journey that requires patience, understanding, and a shared commitment to growth and healing.

While the path to restoring intimacy may be long and complex, it offers the possibility of creating a relationship that is stronger, more resilient, and more fulfilling than before. By facing the challenges head-on, embracing vulnerability, and working together, couples can heal from the wounds of infidelity and forge a new path towards a loving and intimate connection.

Reconnecting Emotionally

Also, infidelity can leave the betrayed partner devastated and emotionally shattered. The path to healing after infidelity is a challenging one, necessitating sincere efforts from both partners involved. While the task of rebuilding trust may seem daunting, one crucial element often overlooked is the significance of reconnecting emotionally. This article delves into the complexities of emotional reconnection as a vital requirement for recovery after infidelity, highlighting its multifaceted nature and the transformative impact it can have on the healing process.

Understanding the Emotional Fallout:
Infidelity inflicts deep emotional wounds on the betrayed partner, often leading to a profound sense of insecurity, diminished self-worth, and a pervasive fear of further betrayal. The pain and anguish experienced can hinder the healing process and create barriers to the possibility of restoration. Emotional disconnection becomes a pervasive issue, with the betrayed partner

guarding their heart, fearing vulnerability, and struggling to trust their unfaithful partner once more.

Reconnecting on an Emotional Level:
Recovery from infidelity demands a concerted effort from both partners to engage in open and honest communication. Reconnecting emotionally requires active listening, empathy, and an unwavering commitment to understanding each other's perspectives. It involves creating a safe space where the betrayed partner can express their pain, anger, and insecurities without judgment or retribution. The unfaithful partner, in turn, must display genuine remorse, taking responsibility for their actions and demonstrating a willingness to rebuild trust.

Rebuilding Trust through Emotional Reconnection:
Trust, once shattered, is challenging to regain. Emotional reconnection serves as the cornerstone for rebuilding trust after infidelity. It involves consistent, transparent, and dependable behavior from

the unfaithful partner, demonstrating their commitment to change. Small acts of kindness, open and respectful communication, and a willingness to be accountable for their actions gradually help rebuild the trust that was lost. Patience and understanding from both partners are crucial during this intricate process, as rebuilding trust takes time and effort.

Addressing Emotional Intimacy:
Beyond trust, emotional reconnection involves reestablishing emotional intimacy. Infidelity often damages the emotional bond between partners, leaving them feeling disconnected and distant. Both partners must actively engage in rebuilding emotional intimacy, understanding that it involves vulnerability, shared experiences, and deep emotional connection. It necessitates nurturing the relationship through quality time spent together, engaging in activities that promote emotional closeness, and expressing love and appreciation for one another.

Navigating Emotional Challenges:
The journey towards emotional reconnection after infidelity is fraught with challenges. The betrayed partner may experience triggers, reminders of the betrayal that elicit intense emotional reactions. These triggers can hinder progress, reinforcing the pain of the past and impeding emotional healing. It is essential for both partners to develop strategies to address these triggers constructively, allowing for open dialogue and mutual support. Professional guidance, such as couples therapy, can provide a safe space to explore and navigate these emotional challenges effectively.

The Transformational Power of Emotional Reconnection:
While the process of emotional reconnection after infidelity may be arduous, the rewards are profound. Through a commitment to rebuilding emotional bonds, both partners have an opportunity to grow individually and as a couple. The betrayed partner can gradually regain their sense of security and

self-worth, finding solace in the genuine efforts of their partner to heal the wounds inflicted. The unfaithful partner, too, can experience personal growth and transformation, developing a deeper understanding of the pain caused and actively working to become a better partner.

Recovering from infidelity is a complex and intricate process, demanding sincere efforts from both partners involved. Emotional reconnection stands as an indispensable requirement for healing after betrayal. By actively engaging in open communication, rebuilding trust, addressing emotional intimacy, and navigating challenges together, both partners can embark on a transformative journey of healing and growth. Through emotional reconnection, a stronger and more resilient relationship can emerge, laying the foundation for a brighter future built on trust, love, and understanding.

Addressing Sexual Issues

Addressing sexual issues after the occurrence of infidelity is a crucial aspect of rebuilding trust and healing in a relationship. Infidelity can have a profound impact on the sexual dynamic between partners, leading to a breakdown in intimacy, emotional connection, and overall satisfaction. Therefore, it becomes imperative to address these sexual issues as part of the recovery process.

One of the primary reasons why addressing sexual issues is vital after infidelity is that the act of cheating often shatters the trust and safety within the relationship. The betrayed partner may experience a range of emotions, including hurt, betrayal, anger, and insecurity. These emotions can significantly affect their willingness to engage in sexual intimacy with their unfaithful partner. It is crucial to acknowledge and validate these feelings before attempting to rebuild the sexual connection.

Moreover, infidelity can introduce a multitude of concerns related to sexual health and safety. The betrayed partner may worry about potential exposure to sexually transmitted infections (STIs) or question the faithfulness of their unfaithful partner. Addressing these concerns requires open and honest communication, along with a commitment to addressing any potential health risks through testing, treatment, and safe sexual practices.

Beyond physical health concerns, the emotional impact of infidelity on a couple's sexual relationship cannot be underestimated. The betrayed partner may experience a diminished sense of self-worth and body image, which can profoundly influence their desire and ability to engage in sexual intimacy. Similarly, the unfaithful partner may grapple with guilt, shame, and self-blame, which can create barriers to fully participating in a healthy sexual relationship. Both partners must navigate these emotional challenges together to restore the emotional and sexual connection.

Furthermore, addressing sexual issues post-infidelity allows couples to explore the underlying causes that contributed to the infidelity. Often, infidelity is a symptom of deeper issues within the relationship, including unresolved conflicts, unmet needs, or emotional disconnection. By delving into these root causes, couples can identify and address the issues that led to the infidelity, working towards establishing a healthier and more fulfilling sexual relationship.

Couples can benefit greatly from seeking professional help when addressing sexual issues after infidelity. A skilled therapist or counselor can provide a safe and neutral space for both partners to express their feelings, fears, and desires surrounding the sexual aspect of their relationship. This professional guidance can help couples navigate through the complexities of rebuilding trust, improving communication, and reintegrating sexual intimacy in a way that is mutually satisfying and respectful.

It is important to note that addressing sexual issues after infidelity does not imply rushing into physical intimacy. Rebuilding trust takes time and requires a gradual progression towards sexual reconnection. Couples may need to establish new boundaries, negotiate consent, and prioritize emotional healing before fully engaging in sexual intimacy. Patience, understanding, and empathy are vital during this process to ensure that both partners feel heard and supported.

In some cases, couples may find it beneficial to explore individual therapy alongside couples therapy to address personal sexual issues that may have contributed to the infidelity. This approach allows each partner to work on their personal growth, healing, and sexual self-discovery. By focusing on individual sexual issues, couples can create a solid foundation for a healthier sexual relationship moving forward.

Conclusively, addressing sexual issues as a requirement for recovery after infidelity is integral to rebuilding trust, emotional connection, and intimacy within a relationship. By acknowledging the impact of infidelity on the sexual dynamic, addressing concerns related to sexual health and safety, navigating the emotional challenges, exploring underlying causes, seeking professional help, and allowing for individual growth, couples can gradually restore and enhance their sexual relationship. The journey towards healing and rebuilding trust takes time, effort, and a commitment from both partners, but it can lead to a more fulfilling and resilient relationship in the long run.

Chapter Five

PROCESSING AND MANAGING GRIEF

Processing and managing grief after infidelity is an essential and intricate aspect of the healing journey for the betrayed partner. Infidelity can bring about profound emotional pain, a sense of loss, and a shattered belief in the stability of the relationship. Consequently, it becomes crucial to navigate the complex emotions associated with grief to achieve personal growth, find closure, and move forward.

When infidelity is discovered, the betrayed partner often experiences a range of intense emotions that parallel the stages of grief. Denial may be the initial response, as the mind struggles to comprehend the betrayal and its implications. Anger soon follows, as feelings of injustice, hurt, and betrayal emerge. Bargaining may arise, as the betrayed partner questions what could have been done differently to prevent the infidelity. Sadness and depression can then settle in, as the profound loss of trust and the realization of shattered dreams take hold. Finally, acceptance becomes a goal, as the betrayed partner strives to come to terms with the reality of the situation and seek a path forward.

Processing grief after infidelity involves creating a safe space for the betrayed partner to express and explore their emotions. This can be achieved through open and honest communication with the unfaithful partner, a trusted friend, or a professional counselor. It is crucial for the betrayed partner to feel heard, validated, and supported as they navigate the tumultuous waves of grief. By acknowledging and giving space to these emotions, healing can begin to take place.

Managing grief after infidelity also requires self-care and self-compassion. Engaging in activities that promote emotional well-being, such as exercise, meditation, journaling, or seeking solace in nature, can provide a sense of grounding and release. Self-compassion involves treating oneself with kindness and understanding, recognizing that healing takes time and that it is natural to experience a wide range of emotions. This self-care and self-compassion create a foundation for healing and resilience in the face of grief.

Furthermore, seeking professional support can be immensely beneficial when managing grief after infidelity. Therapists or counselors experienced in working with couples dealing with infidelity can provide guidance, tools, and coping strategies to navigate the grieving process. These professionals can also help facilitate effective communication between partners, addressing underlying issues, and exploring the possibilities of forgiveness and rebuilding trust.

The grieving process after infidelity may also involve reevaluating one's personal values, needs, and boundaries. The experience of betrayal can bring about a profound shift in perspective, prompting the betrayed partner to reflect on their own desires, aspirations, and expectations in relationships. Setting and asserting healthy boundaries becomes crucial during this time, as it allows the betrayed partner to protect their emotional well-being and ensure that their needs are met moving forward.

Another important aspect of managing grief after infidelity is finding meaning and purpose in the experience. The betrayed partner may benefit from reframing the pain and loss as an opportunity for personal growth and self-discovery. Through introspection, they can identify areas for personal development, such as building resilience, improving communication skills, or cultivating a stronger sense of self. **This process of finding meaning allows the betrayed partner to transform their grief into a catalyst for positive change and personal empowerment.**

It is important to note that managing grief after infidelity is not a linear process. Emotions may fluctuate, and setbacks are common. The betrayed partner may experience moments of progress and clarity, only to be followed by waves of sadness, anger, or confusion. Patience, self-compassion, and understanding are essential during these times. Each individual's grief journey is unique, and it is crucial to honor and respect the process, allowing oneself to heal at their own pace.

By acknowledging and exploring the emotions associated with grief, engaging in self-care and self-compassion, seeking professional support, reevaluating personal values and boundaries, and finding meaning in the experience, the betrayed partner can gradually navigate through the grieving process and find healing.

Throughout this journey, it is important for the betrayed partner to practice self-forgiveness and avoid blaming themselves for the infidelity. Infidelity is a complex issue influenced by multiple factors, and it is not solely the responsibility of the betrayed partner. By recognizing this, the individual can release feelings of guilt or shame that may hinder their healing process.

Additionally, the unfaithful partner also plays a crucial role in supporting the grieving process. They must take responsibility for their actions, show genuine remorse, and actively participate in the healing journey. This involves listening to the betrayed partner's feelings, demonstrating empathy, and being transparent and trustworthy in their actions moving forward. Rebuilding trust is a gradual process that requires consistent effort and a commitment to open communication.

Couples who are navigating grief after infidelity may benefit from engaging in relationship repair strategies. This can involve attending couples therapy or participating in relationship workshops specifically designed for couples healing from infidelity. These interventions provide a structured environment for both partners to address underlying issues, improve communication, rebuild trust, and work towards restoring the relationship.

It is important to acknowledge that not all relationships can or should be salvaged after infidelity. In some cases, despite efforts to heal and rebuild, the emotional damage may be irreparable. In such situations, the grieving process becomes essential in order to come to terms with the loss of the relationship and move towards personal growth and new beginnings.

Ultimately, processing and managing grief after infidelity is a deeply individual process, and there is no universal timeline for healing. Each person's journey is unique, and it is essential to honor their emotions, needs, and pace. By embracing the complexities of grief, seeking support, and engaging in self-care, individuals can find strength, resilience, and a renewed sense of self as they navigate the challenging aftermath of infidelity.

Managing Post Traumatic Stress

Infidelity can be a very devastating experience, shaking the foundation of trust in a relationship and leaving long-lasting emotional wounds. For the betrayed partner, the aftermath of infidelity can result in a range of intense emotions, including anger, betrayal, sadness, and insecurity. In some cases, these emotional responses can evolve into post-traumatic stress disorder (PTSD) symptoms, which further complicate the healing process. This article explores the complexities of managing post-traumatic stress after infidelity and offers strategies to support individuals in their journey towards healing.

Understanding Post-Traumatic Stress after Infidelity:

Post-traumatic stress is typically associated with traumatic events such as physical assault, natural disasters, or combat experiences. However, infidelity can also trigger symptoms akin to PTSD due to the profound impact it has on one's sense of safety, identity, and trust in others. The betrayed partner may experience intrusive thoughts, flashbacks to the discovery of the affair, hyperarousal, hypervigilance, and a persistent sense of emotional distress.

Recognizing and Validating Emotional Responses:
The first step in managing post-traumatic stress after infidelity is recognizing and validating the range of emotions experienced by the betrayed partner. It is crucial to acknowledge that these emotions are a normal response to a significant betrayal and not a sign of weakness. Encouraging open and honest communication within the relationship can help foster a safe space for the betrayed partner to express their feelings without judgment or blame.

Seeking Professional Support:
Dealing with post-traumatic stress after infidelity can be an overwhelming and complex process. Seeking professional support from a therapist or counselor

experienced in trauma and relationship issues can provide invaluable guidance and assistance. Therapy offers a confidential and non-judgmental environment where individuals can explore their emotions, gain insights into the impact of the infidelity, and develop coping strategies to manage post-traumatic stress symptoms effectively.

Rebuilding Trust and Establishing Safety:
Rebuilding trust is a crucial aspect of healing after infidelity and managing post-traumatic stress. The unfaithful partner must take responsibility for their actions, demonstrate genuine remorse, and engage in consistent, open, and transparent communication. Re-establishing safety within the relationship involves creating clear boundaries, implementing mutually agreed-upon safeguards, and addressing any underlying issues that may have contributed to the infidelity.

Self-Care and Self-Compassion:
Taking care of oneself is paramount when managing post-traumatic stress after infidelity. Engaging in self-care activities

such as exercise, practicing mindfulness or meditation, pursuing hobbies, and spending time with supportive friends and family can promote emotional well-being. Cultivating self-compassion is equally important, as it involves treating oneself with kindness, understanding, and forgiveness, acknowledging that healing takes time and effort.

Processing and Grieving:
The betrayed partner may go through a grieving process similar to that experienced after the death of a loved one. This process involves acknowledging the loss of the relationship as it once was, processing the associated emotions, and gradually accepting the new reality. Allowing oneself to grieve and seeking support from loved ones or support groups can aid in the healing journey and help manage post-traumatic stress symptoms.

Communication and Rebuilding Intimacy:
Rebuilding intimacy and restoring emotional connection after infidelity can be challenging but is vital for healing. Open

and honest communication is key, as both partners need to express their needs, fears, and concerns. Engaging in couples therapy can facilitate this process, providing a structured environment for dialogue, conflict resolution, and the rebuilding of emotional intimacy.

Dealing with Triggers, Intrusive Thoughts, and Reminders

The discovery of infidelity in a relationship can lead to a range of overwhelming emotions and psychological distress. Even after the initial shock subsides, the betrayed partner may continue to face triggers, intrusive thoughts, and reminders that intensify their pain and hinder the healing process. This article explores the complexities of dealing with triggers and intrusive thoughts after infidelity and provides strategies to effectively navigate and manage these challenging experiences.

Understanding Triggers, Intrusive Thoughts, and Reminders:

Triggers are stimuli that evoke emotional or physiological responses linked to a traumatic event, such as the discovery of infidelity. These triggers can be external, such as encountering a particular location or object associated with the affair, or internal, arising from thoughts, memories, or emotional states. Intrusive thoughts, on the other hand, are unwelcome and distressing thoughts that spontaneously occur, often replaying the betrayal in the mind. Reminders are external cues or situations that bring the infidelity to the forefront of consciousness.

Identifying Triggers and Patterns:
The first step in dealing with triggers, intrusive thoughts, and reminders is to identify the specific stimuli or situations that evoke a strong emotional response. This may include places, songs, photographs, or conversations that remind the betrayed partner of the affair. Recognizing patterns in the triggers can help anticipate and prepare for potential encounters, empowering the individual to respond in a more controlled and self-compassionate manner.

Developing Coping Strategies:
Once triggers and patterns are identified, it is important to develop personalized coping strategies to manage the emotional impact they have. Strategies may include deep

breathing exercises, mindfulness techniques, grounding exercises, or engaging in a distracting activity. Experimenting with different coping mechanisms can help find what works best for the individual, providing a sense of control and relief during triggering moments.

Challenging Intrusive Thoughts:
Intrusive thoughts can be distressing and persistent, causing significant emotional turmoil. Challenging these thoughts involves recognizing them as intrusive and actively questioning their accuracy and validity. It is important to remind oneself that these thoughts do not define reality and are a natural response to the trauma of infidelity. Engaging in cognitive restructuring techniques, such as reframing negative thoughts or replacing them with more positive and realistic ones, can help reduce their intensity and frequency over time.

Establishing Boundaries and Self-Care:

Creating and maintaining boundaries is crucial when dealing with triggers and reminders. This may involve setting limits on exposure to certain situations or individuals that consistently trigger distressing emotions. Prioritizing self-care is equally important, as it provides the necessary emotional and physical support to navigate challenging moments. Engaging in activities that promote relaxation, self-soothing, and self-compassion can help individuals build resilience and reduce the impact of triggers and intrusive thoughts.

Communicating with the Partner:

Open and honest communication with the unfaithful partner is essential when managing triggers and intrusive thoughts. Sharing one's emotional experience and discussing specific triggers can foster understanding and empathy. The unfaithful partner can play a supportive role by actively listening, expressing remorse, and respecting the boundaries established by the betrayed partner. Jointly developing strategies to manage triggers within the relationship can promote healing and rebuild trust.

Seeking Professional Support:
Dealing with triggers, intrusive thoughts, and reminders after infidelity can be overwhelming on your own sometimes. If push comes to shove, seeking professional support from a therapist or counselor trained in trauma and relationship issues can provide guidance and validation. Therapy helps to offer a safe space to process emotions, learn coping skills, and work towards post-traumatic growth. Also, therapists have various specialized techniques they employ like Eye Movement Desensitization and Reprocessing (EMDR) to help individuals effectively manage and reduce the impact of triggers and intrusive thoughts.

Chapter Summary
Dealing with triggers, intrusive thoughts, and reminders after infidelity is a complex and deeply personal journey. By understanding these experiences,

identifying triggers, developing coping strategies, establishing boundaries, and seeking support, individuals can gradually regain control over their emotional well-being. With time, patience, and self-compassion, it is possible to heal and move towards a renewed sense of self and trust in future relationships.

Chapter Six

A PRACTICAL APPROACH

This chapter hopes to prescribe certain practical steps to be taken by both the betrayed partner and the unfaithful one. No matter how much the hurt is on the spouse cheated on, the fact remains that the relationship is made up of two entities. Therefore, there are roles to be played by either party.

For the sake of this chapter, the unfaithful partner would be frequently referred to as "the betrayer" while the partner cheated on would be addressed as "the betrayed".

Tasks for The Betrayer (Unfaithful Partner)

Dear unfaithful partner!

Infidelity is a deeply painful experience that can shatter the trust and foundation of any relationship. However, with genuine remorse, commitment, and a willingness to change, it is possible for you to take crucial steps toward rebuilding trust and restoring your damaged relationship. We would be exploring some very necessary tasks that you should undertake in order to embark on a journey of healing, growth, and reconciliation.

1. Acceptance and Accountability:
Accepting personal responsibility and acknowledging the immense pain caused is the foundational task for you in your quest to restore trust. It requires an honest and introspective examination of one's motives, choices, and the impact it had on the partner.

Minimizing or justifying the betrayal should be avoided, as it hinders the healing process.

By taking accountability, the betrayer demonstrates a genuine desire to rebuild the relationship.

2. Open and Transparent
   Communication:

Rebuilding trust demands open, honest, and consistent communication. You should create a safe space for your betrayed partner to express their emotions, concerns, and questions. Engaging in active listening allows your betrayed partner to feel heard and validated. Transparency becomes paramount, since you need to provide answers and reassurances whenever necessary. Establishing effective communication channels helps rebuild the foundation of trust, promoting healing and understanding.

3. Patience and Empathy:

Patience becomes a virtue for the betrayer, as they navigate the complex emotional journey of their betrayed partner, offering unwavering support and understanding. Your betrayed partner may experience a range of emotions, including anger, sadness, and insecurity. It is crucial for the betrayer to acknowledge and validate these emotions without defensiveness or impatience. Cultivating empathy allows the betrayer to truly grasp the magnitude of their partner's emotional turmoil, paving the way for healing and reconciliation.

4. Genuine Remorse and Apology:
Expressing genuine remorse is an essential task for the betrayer seeking to restore the relationship. A heartfelt apology, devoid of excuses, is crucial for the healing process. You should demonstrate a deep understanding of the pain caused, the impact on your partner, and a sincere commitment to change.

It is important to emphasize that actions speak louder than words, and the betrayer's subsequent behavior should align with their apology.

5. Personal Reflection and
    Self-Improvement:
In order to restore the relationship, the unfaithful partner must embark on a journey of self-reflection and personal growth. This involves identifying the underlying causes that led to the infidelity, such as personal insecurities, emotional disconnection, or unresolved issues.

Engaging in this form of introspection and self-reflection would allow the defaulting partner to delve into the root causes of the infidelity, address personal shortcomings and seek avenues for growth. By actively pursuing personal development, they show their commitment to change and creating a better foundation for the restored relationship.

Tasks For The Betrayed

Dear Heartbroken Partner!

Discovering infidelity in a relationship can be a profoundly painful experience, leaving you (the betrayed partner) devastated and uncertain about the future. While the focus is often on the tasks for the betrayer in rebuilding the relationship, it is equally important for the betrayed individual to undertake essential tasks for their own healing and to contribute to the process of rebuilding trust. Like I will always say, relationships are a two-way street!

We would be exploring the tasks that the betrayed partner can engage in to navigate the challenging aftermath of infidelity and work towards personal growth and relationship recovery.

1. Allowing and Expressing Emotions: The first crucial task for the betrayed partner is to acknowledge and allow themselves to experience the range of emotions that arise from the betrayal. It is natural to feel anger, sadness, betrayal, and

a profound sense of loss. Instead of suppressing these emotions, it is important to create a safe space to express and process them. This might involve seeking support from friends, family, or a therapist who can provide validation and guidance during this difficult time.

2. Establishing Boundaries:
Setting clear boundaries is essential for the betrayed partner's emotional well-being and self-respect. This involves determining what is acceptable and unacceptable behavior from the betrayer moving forward. Communicating these boundaries assertively and effectively is crucial for rebuilding trust and protecting oneself from further harm. Boundaries may include stipulations regarding communication, social interactions, and actions that can help regain a sense of security.

3. Engaging in Self-Care:
Self-care is paramount for the betrayed partner during the healing process. Taking care of physical, emotional, and mental well-being is crucial for regaining strength

and resilience. Engaging in activities that bring joy, practicing mindfulness or meditation, exercising regularly, and maintaining a healthy lifestyle can contribute to the process of healing and rebuilding self-esteem.

4. Seeking Support and Therapy:
The betrayed partner should consider seeking professional help or joining a support group specifically tailored for individuals dealing with infidelity. Therapy can provide a safe and non-judgmental space to process emotions, gain insights, and develop coping strategies. Support groups offer the opportunity to connect with others who have experienced similar situations, providing a sense of validation, understanding, and guidance.

5. Rebuilding Self-Identity and Trust:
Infidelity can significantly impact one's self-identity and sense of trust. The betrayed partner should focus on rebuilding their self-worth and reclaiming their identity separate from the infidelity. Engaging in activities that foster personal

growth, pursuing hobbies or interests, and rediscovering personal strengths can aid in regaining confidence and rebuilding trust in oneself.

6. Open Communication and Seeking Answers:

Open communication with the betrayer is essential for the betrayed partner's healing process. Expressing concerns, asking questions, and seeking honest answers can help create clarity and understanding. However, it is important to approach these conversations with emotional preparedness and to establish healthy communication patterns that promote mutual respect and empathy.

7. Gradual Trust-Building:

Rebuilding trust is a gradual process and requires active participation from both partners. The betrayed partner should allow the betrayer opportunities to demonstrate their commitment to change and rebuild trust. However, it is important to set realistic expectations and monitor progress over time. Trust-building exercises, such as gradually reintroducing shared activities or implementing transparency measures, can aid in rebuilding trust in a structured and manageable manner.

Funny how the betrayed partner gets more tasks than the other? Of course, it is!

Well, the focus remains on restoring the relationship and for this to be effectively achieved, **the emotional well-being of the hurt partner must be seriously considered.**

EPILOGUE

While it's true that no relationship remains the same after infidelity has been discovered, it is also true that some relationships get restored, and become even stronger in the aftermath.

This may or may not apply to your relationship but it is very important to attempt to fix it. Traditionally, the onus is on the cheating partner to try to make things right, but as an emotionally-mature spouse, you should put in your own quota.

Don't let a one-time act destroy your relationship.

Always rooting for your success!

www.ingramcontent.com/pod-product-compliance
Lightning Source LLC
LaVergne TN
LVHW021208080625
813324LV00009B/674